MW01127800

AWESOME ATHLETES

DAVID BECKHAM

Jill C. Wheeler

ABDO Publishing Company

visit us at
www.abdopublishing.com

Published by ABDO Publishing Company, 4940 Viking Drive, Edina, Minnesota 55435.
Copyright © 2007 by Abdo Consulting Group, Inc. International copyrights reserved in all
countries. No part of this book may be reproduced in any form without written permission from
the publisher. The Checkerboard Library™ is a trademark and logo of ABDO Publishing
Company.

Printed in the United States.

Cover Photo: Getty Images
Interior Photos: AP/WideWorld p. 4; Corbis pp. 7, 9, 10, 16, 17, 19, 21, 22, 23, 25, 27, 28-29, 31;
  Getty Images pp. 5, 13, 14, 15, 24

Series Coordinator: Rochelle Baltzer
Editors: Rochelle Baltzer, Stephanie Hedlund
Art Direction: Neil Klinepier

Library of Congress Cataloging-in-Publication Data

Wheeler, Jill C., 1964-
  David Beckham / Jill C. Wheeler.
     p. cm. -- (Awesome athletes)
  Includes index.
  ISBN-10 1-59928-304-2
  ISBN-13 978-1-59928-304-3
  1. Beckham, David, 1975- 2. Soccer players--England--Biography--Juvenile literature. 3.
Celebrities--England--Biography--Juvenile literature. I. Title. II. Series.

GV942.7.B432W484 2007
796.334092--dc22
                                                          2005035427

Contents

David Beckham

David Beckham is possibly the world's most popular soccer player. He is best known for his kicking skills. His amazing kicks have helped this **midfielder** lead his team to many victories.

Beckham's curving kicks have gained him fame well beyond soccer fans. In 2002, *Bend It Like Beckham* was released in the **United Kingdom**. This movie is about a young Indian girl who dreams of playing professional soccer. In the film, Beckham is one of her heroes.

Beckham is not only a soccer star. He is also an international celebrity. Beckham's name appears in news stories around the globe. Not all the stories are about soccer, either. Many cover the star's personal life.

Beckham wrote a book about his life. This autobiography was published in 2003.

For as long as he can remember, all Beckham has ever wanted to do is play soccer. Even as a child, he said he wanted to be "a famous footballer." Beckham has played professionally since he was 17 years old. Today, he also enjoys helping young people learn about soccer and improve their skills.

Beckham has always had a love for cars. Today, this soccer star is reported to own 15 luxury cars! Among them are two Ferraris, a Lamborghini, and a Bentley.

Discovering Soccer

David Beckham was born on May 2, 1975, in Leytonstone, England. He grew up in Chingford. Both towns are near London, England.

David's parents are Ted and Sandra Beckham. Ted was a repairman, and Sandra was a hairdresser. David has two sisters. Lynne is three years older than him, and Joanne is five years younger.

Soccer has been a part of David's life from the start. When David was young, his father played for a local team. And almost as soon as David could walk, Ted gave his son a soccer ball.

Ted's favorite soccer **club** was Manchester United. David quickly became a United fan, too. Soon, David was saying he would play for them when he grew up.

Ted did his part to help his son make that dream a reality. He played soccer with David nearly every day. And, Ted eventually quit playing on his team to spend more time coaching his son. David says he learned many important skills from his father.

David enjoyed activities other than soccer, too. He bicycled, roller-skated, and played in the park with friends. David also liked to draw. He recalls spending hours copying Disney cartoon characters from comics. Later, he began drawing people playing soccer.

David regularly practiced football, or soccer, at local parks with his father. Football is what people outside the United States call soccer.

Getting Noticed

David was seven years old when he started playing soccer with the Ridgeway Rovers. The Rovers coaches were stern with the team. No player was allowed in a game if he had missed that week's practice. The coaches also made sure that no single player got too much attention. Soon, their team started winning.

David was one of the smaller players on the Rovers. He often played against kids who were bigger than he was. Ted reminded David that if he was pushed down, he had to get up and keep going. Young David followed this advice. Now, David believes those experiences made him a better player.

In summer 1985, David attended a weeklong soccer camp. The Bobby Charlton Soccer School attracted young players from around the world. David loved playing soccer at the camp, but he also felt homesick.

However, the following summer David decided to try the camp again. This time, he did very well. At the end of the week, he even won the skills competition! His prize was a trip to a two-week soccer camp in Barcelona, Spain.

David enjoyed going to Spain. Meanwhile, Manchester United **scouts** had noticed him. David kept in contact with them. And on his thirteenth birthday, he accepted an offer with the **club** he once dreamed of playing on.

David had wanted to play soccer for Manchester United since he was a child. Little did he know that he would go on to become one of the team's most valuable players.

Manchester At Last

At 13 years old, David was too young to play soccer professionally. So, his first two years with United were in its development league. He traveled to Manchester several times each year for training sessions. Back home, he continued to play with the Ridgeway Rovers. And, he attended high school in Chingford.

Next, David became a member of United's youth team. That meant moving from London to Manchester. But, David was too young for his own apartment. So, the team arranged for him to live with a family in Manchester.

In September 1992, David first played with the professional United team. He was put in as a substitute for another United player. David did well, but there were more experienced players on the team.

During the 1994–1995 season, United loaned David to a **club** called Preston North End for a month. David was sad to leave United at first. But by the end of the month, he enjoyed playing for Preston. He didn't want to go back to United.

However, United wanted David back. In summer 1995, several players left United for other clubs. David and a few other young players became their replacements. United fans wondered if the new players were up to the challenge. David wondered, too.

Opposite Page: Manchester's Great Northern Square is surrounded by shops and restaurants. Before David moved into his own apartment, he lived with several different families in Manchester.

First Goal

David scored his first professional goal for United in August 1995. He remembers the 1995–1996 season as a time of growth. He finally moved into his own town house, and he got his first car. But the following season, David scored a goal that changed his life.

In August 1996, Manchester United was playing Wimbledon. David received a pass just inside his team's half of the field. He kicked the ball, and the crowd anxiously watched it sail toward the edge of Wimbledon's goal. But then it curved back, flew over Wimbledon's goalkeeper, and crashed into the net for a goal.

David had scored from nearly 60 yards (55 m) away! The shot made history. It also turned David into a celebrity. Suddenly, it seemed as though everyone knew about his incredible kick.

A few days later, David landed a spot on the English national team. This team represents England in international competitions, such as the World Cup.

The match against Wimbledon on August 17, 1996, jump-started David's soccer career.

The English national team in June 1997. David is in the front row on the left.

During the rest of the 1996–1997 season, David scored 11 more goals. His achievements helped him win the Professional Footballers' Association Young Player of the Year award in 1997.

Soccer fans were starting to notice David. Meanwhile, David had noticed someone, too. He had seen a music video of the Spice Girls, a popular singing group at the time. His favorite Spice Girl was the one called Posh.

David decided he had to meet Posh. It wasn't long before his wish came true. He met her after one of his games and learned her real name was Victoria Adams. The two began dating shortly after that.

David and Victoria got engaged in January 1998. English people have nicknamed them "Posh and Becks."

THE MAKING OF AN AWESOME ATHLETE

Many people consider David Beckham to be the most famous soccer player in the world.

1975	1986	1988	1998
Born on May 2 in Leytonstone, England	Wins skills competition at Bobby Charlton Soccer School	Signs with Manchester United	Plays in first World Cup

How Awesome Is He?

Beckham is known for his ability to "bend" a kick so that the ball curves in the air to go around defending players. Some people think Beckham has unusual knee and ankle joints that allow him to do that. He often uses these kicks to assist teammates in scoring.

Player	Assists (2005–2006 season)
David Beckham	**10**
Zinedine Zidane	6
Raúl González Blanco	3
Ronaldo Luis Nazário de Lima	2

DAVID BECKHAM

TEAM: REAL MADRID
NUMBER: 23
POSITION: MIDFIELDER
HEIGHT: 5 FEET, 11 INCHES
WEIGHT: 163 POUNDS

2000	**2002**	**2003**	**2006**
Captains England's national team for the first time	Plays in second World Cup	Signs with Real Madrid	Plays in third World Cup

- ⚽ **Helped Manchester United win the English Premier League Championship six times**
- ⚽ **Became an Officer of the Order of the British Empire in 2003 for his contribution to sports in Britain**
- ⚽ **Four out of every five Real Madrid shirts sold carry Beckham's name and number**

Highlights

World Cup Disaster

Beckham's career was going remarkably well. As a member of England's national team, Beckham played in the 1998 World Cup. The World Cup is an international soccer tournament held every four years by the Fédération Internationale de Football Association (FIFA).

During the tournament, Beckham played in England's game against Romania. Then, he made a **free kick** in England's game against Colombia. This was his first World Cup goal. England went on to win the match 2–0.

On June 30, England took on Argentina. Beckham's game went well until the second half. Then, Argentina's team captain, Diego Simeone, crashed into Beckham. Beckham fell to the ground. While he was down, Simeone pretended to ruffle Beckham's hair. Beckham lost his temper and angrily flicked his leg up at Simeone.

Simeone fell to the ground dramatically. Beckham was sure he had barely touched Simeone. Yet, he knew many international soccer players pretend to fall hard to win penalties for their side. It appeared Simeone had done just that.

The referee called a **foul** on Simeone for pushing Beckham over. However, he removed Beckham from the game for tripping Simeone. England lost the game. This meant they were out of the World Cup. Many fans were angry with Beckham. They believed England would have won had he not been thrown out of the game.

Argentina and England have what Beckham describes as one of the oldest and greatest soccer rivalries of all time. Here, Beckham reacts after being called out of the game.

A Hero Again

After the incident, Beckham felt like the entire country hated him. He publicly apologized for his mistake, but it did not seem to help. Fans booed him whenever he had the ball. He also received threats. To stay safe, Beckham started the 1998–1999 season under police protection.

However, Beckham slowly began to win back his fans that season. With his help, Manchester United won three championships. This is known in the soccer world as a treble victory. His marriage to Victoria and the birth of their first son, Brooklyn, seemed to help, too.

In November 2000, Beckham captained the English national team for the first time. The following season brought even more success. In October 2001, Beckham made a **free kick** in the final moments of a match against Greece. His tie-breaking goal gave England a place in the 2002 World Cup.

Beckham was back in favor. Before the World Cup began, Beckham signed a three-year contract with United. His salary tripled!

Opposite Page: Beckham gives two-year-old Brooklyn a kiss after Manchester won the Premier League Championship in May 2001. The Premier League is the top level of football in England. It is made up of 20 clubs.

The World Cup was set to begin on May 31, 2002. In April, Beckham was tackled during a match against Argentina. The fall broke a bone in his foot.

English soccer fans were relieved when doctors cleared Beckham to play. He was just in time for the tournament!

During England's World Cup match against Argentina, Beckham scored a goal in the forty-

Beckham scored against Argentina in the 2002 World Cup. He helped England make it to the quarterfinals!

fourth minute of the first half. England won 1–0. Beckham was again a hero. Sports commentators agreed his game had become more mature and professional.

Opposite Page: As Beckham gained popularity, people looked to him for more than his soccer skills. He also became known for his personal fashion sense.

Move to Madrid

In June 2003, Manchester United agreed to sell Beckham to Real (ray-AHL) Madrid, a Spanish **club**. Beckham signed a four-year contract with Real Madrid that was worth $41 million.

Real Madrid in September 2004

In signing Beckham, Real Madrid hoped to form a dream team. Beckham joined soccer superstars Luis Figo, Zinedine Zidane, and Ronaldo Luis Nazário de Lima. Beckham was excited to be part of a team with such a proud history. He was also eager to move to a new country and learn a new language. And, he felt it was a good opportunity for his family.

Beckham has continued his style of play with Real Madrid. His strengths are **free kicks**, **corner kicks**, and some long passes. Unlike many other players, Beckham rarely **heads** the ball. And though he does not score much, Beckham is a fearless defender.

In July 2005, Real Madrid traveled to Los Angeles, California. There, they played against Major League Soccer team the Los Angeles Galaxy. Some 30,000 fans attended the match. Real Madrid won 2–0. The game marked the end of Real Madrid's United States visit in their World Tour 2005.

Beckham and Real Madrid teammate Figo in action. Beckham continues to practice kicking to sharpen his skills.

Beckham Today

David Beckham remains one of the world's best-known soccer players. His contract with Real Madrid ends in 2007. Some people think Beckham may play for a U.S. team after that. If so, he might make the sport more popular in the United States.

Off the field, David and Victoria Beckham have three sons. Their names are Brooklyn, Romeo, and Cruz. Beckham loves to play soccer with his boys. Like his father, he introduced his sons to soccer almost as soon as they could walk.

In 2005, Beckham opened his own soccer school. The David Beckham Academy aims to give children the same chance that Beckham feels privileged to have had. The academy is located in both England and California.

Beckham also spends time making appearances for his corporate **sponsors**. He has been a spokesperson for many brands, including Pepsi, Brylcreem, Adidas, and Gillette.

In 2006, Beckham played for England in the World Cup once again. However, England lost their quarterfinal match against Portugal. But Beckham had scored a goal in the

Each year, England's David Beckham Academy welcomes about 15,000 boys and girls ages 8 to 15. About 10,000 of them receive the opportunity free of charge.

previous game against Ecuador. This made him England's first player to score a goal in three World Cups!

Beckham still hopes to help England win a World Cup someday. In the meantime, he plans to continue playing soccer. "Football is my life," he said. "I want to keep going as long as I can."

Glossary

club - a soccer team.

corner kick - a free kick that is awarded to an attacker when a defender plays the ball out-of-bounds. It is taken from a corner of a soccer field.

foul - when a player breaks the rules in a game or a sport.

free kick - a kick awarded to a team when its opponent has committed a foul. No opposing players may interfere with the kick.

head - to pass or shoot a soccer ball in the air with one's head.

midfielder - a soccer player who controls and passes the ball to link defensive and offensive players. Midfielders both defend and attack for their teams.

scout - someone sent to discover new talent, such as athletes or entertainers.

sponsor - someone who pays for a program or an activity in return for promotion of a particular product or brand.

United Kingdom - the united countries of England, Scotland, Wales, and Northern Ireland.

Web Sites

To learn more about David Beckham, visit ABDO Publishing Company on the World Wide Web at **www.abdopublishing.com**. Web sites about Beckham are featured on our Book Links page. These links are routinely monitored and updated to provide the most current information available.

Index